A Young Citizen's Guide to News Literacy

WHAT IS BIAS?

Danielle Haynes

PowerKiDS press
New York

Published in 2019 by The Rosen Publishing Group, Inc.
29 East 21st Street, New York, NY 10010

First Edition

Editor: Jill Keppeler
Book Design: Reann Nye

Photo Credits: Cover simonkr/E+/Getty Images; p. 5 g-stockstudio/Shutterstock.com; pp. 7, 9 GaudiLab/Shutterstock.com; p. 11 Rawpixel.com/Shutterstock.com; p. 12 Pressmaster/Shutterstock.com; p. 13 Flamingo Images/Shutterstock.com; p. 15 Maria Dryfhout/Shutterstock.com; p. 16 wellphoto/Shutterstock.com; p. 17 FrameStockFootages/Shutterstock.com; p. 19 Pixsooz/Shutterstock.com; p. 21 PeopleImages/E+/Getty Images; pp. 23, 29 Image Source/Getty Images; p. 24 Chip Somodevilla/x Getty Images News/Getty Images; p. 25 2p2play/Shutterstock.com; p. 27 Westend61/Getty Images; pp. 28, 30 Monkey Business Images/Shutterstock.com.

Library of Congress Cataloging-in-Publication Data

Names: Haynes, Danielle, author.
Title: What is bias? / Danielle Haynes.
Description: New York : PowerKids Press, [2019] | Series: A young citizen's guide to news literacy | Includes index.
Identifiers: LCCN 2018027756| ISBN 9781538346228 (library bound) | ISBN 9781538346204 (pbk.) | ISBN 9781538346211 (6 pack)
Subjects: LCSH: Journalism–Objectivity–Juvenile literature. | Journalism–Juvenile literature.
Classification: LCC PN4784.O24 H39 2019 | DDC 302.23–dc23
LC record available at https://lccn.loc.gov/2018027756

Manufactured in the United States of America

CPSIA Compliance Information: Batch #CWPK19. For Further Information contact Rosen Publishing, New York, New York at 1-800-237-9932

CONTENTS

A POINT OF VIEW

Bias is a tendency to believe that some ideas or views are better than others. Everyone has bias. However, bias in the media refers to the way opinions and **prejudices** can influence a news story. This happens when the views of the reporter, editor, or even the owner of a news organization seep into a news story. News reports shouldn't have opinion, only facts.

Bias can be subtle, or not obvious. It can also be very obvious. When it happens, it can influence how the reader understands a story. If, for example, a reporter agrees with a new law, they may only write about its positive effects. That may lead the reader to feel positive about the new law as well, even if they wouldn't have otherwise. However, the reader doesn't have a full picture.

BREAKING NEWS

While news articles shouldn't have opinion in them, you can expect to read plenty on the opinion or editorial pages of a newspaper. These are the pages where writers and readers can share their personal views.

It's important to be able to tell when bias is affecting a news article or a piece on television or radio news. If it's a pattern, it's a problem.

JOURNALISTS AND BIAS

One of the first lessons students of **journalism** learn is the importance of objectivity. An objective news article or broadcast is free of bias and prejudice—it will be **neutral** and fair in the way it reports the facts.

No person in this world is completely objective. The trick for journalists is to recognize their own biases and challenge their own assumptions. They must question and **verify** all information they use in a news article or broadcast to make sure it's correct and doesn't just back up their own beliefs.

At the same time, good news consumers need to be sure they're not just reading or watching news that backs up their own biases. Before you decide a news outlet is biased, consider—is the bias really coming from you?

BREAKING NEWS

Someone may say only good things about a politician they like and ignore the politician's bad qualities. (Or the other way around.) This is called bias by **omission**—when someone leaves out details in order to promote their own opinions.

Even though journalists may have personal opinions about the topic they're reporting on, they should make sure their own biases don't damage the **credibility** of their work.

LOADED LANGUAGE

While bias can be easy to spot in a news article or broadcast, sometimes it's subtler, with the use of loaded or editorializing language. A news reporter usually won't say outright if they like or dislike a political candidate or an organization they're writing about, but their opinions can seep into their stories.

To avoid this, reporters must be specific in their language. They shouldn't describe a new public building as "too expensive." That's opinion. Instead, they should just report the facts: "It will cost $10 million."

Likewise, reporters shouldn't include details unnecessary to the story. A profile about a new female mayor shouldn't focus on her clothes or hairstyle. A profile about a male mayor isn't likely to include those details. This is called gender bias. It downplays the woman's accomplishments by leaning on traditional gender **stereotypes**. Those details don't affect the mayor's job.

Loaded language can influence a reader and should be confined to the opinion pages of a newspaper. News articles should steer clear of opinionated language.

SPOT THE DIFFERENCE

Compare these headlines about a new refugee law:

- "Law only allows 110,000 refugees to enter U.S. each year." The use of the word "only" implies the writer thinks the number is too low.
- "New law will flood U.S. with refugees." The word "flood" is an **exaggeration** and implies the writer thinks the number is too high.
- "U.S. to admit 110,000 refugees each year." This headline simply states the facts.

ABOVE THE FOLD

The stories a news outlet chooses to cover and the ways in which editors or producers choose to present these stories also can reflect bias. "Story selection" refers to which stories a news organization decides to report on and which it chooses to skip. "Placement" is where the story appears—stories at the top of the front page or at the beginning of a news broadcast are considered to be the most important.

If a news organization regularly skips topics that make one political party look bad or hides them in the back pages of a newspaper or much later in a broadcast, it may be biased in favor of that party.

Bias by placement also occurs if a reporter highlights one view at the beginning of a news article or broadcast and downplays another at the end.

BREAKING NEWS

In a newspaper, the most important news stories of the day go on the front page above the fold. Headlines above the fold can easily be seen in newsstands and grab attention.

If a news website buries the link to a big story of the day at the bottom of its home page, readers might question the organization's motives.

CORPORATE BIAS

If the placement of a story—or lack of a story—in a news outlet seems fishy, it might be time to consider who owns the news organization. The companies that own news outlets shouldn't try to influence what's reported for their own gain.

Consider your local newspaper. Who owns it? Is it a smaller paper owned by one person, or is it one of many outlets owned by a company? Do the people in charge have interests (financial investments or political ties) that may influence how topics are presented in their newspapers?

For example, it's the job of the editors at the *Washington Post* to make sure they use objectivity when reporting about Amazon.com—or laws that affect Amazon—because the same man, Jeff Bezos, owns both companies.

Just because corporate owners don't work in the same newsroom with reporters and editors doesn't mean they can't have an effect on what's reported in a newspaper or TV broadcast.

GOVERNMENT-RUN NEWS

In some countries, the government owns most, if not all, of the media outlets. This typically happens in countries, such as China and Russia, where the government tries to control the information its citizens consume. Nations with state media—also called state-run media—seek to have only news favorable to the leader or political party in power. Some U.S. news outlets, such as Voice of America and National Public Radio, receive some public funding, but the government doesn't control them.

ADVERTISING BIAS

One example of corporate bias is advertising bias. This is when the owner of a news outlet pressures reporters to cover a story in a way favorable to advertisers. This could be **unethical** but relatively harmless—for instance, reporting on the grand opening of a restaurant whose owners bought an advertisement in that day's newspaper.

Some cases, though, may keep needed information from the public. A newspaper may cave to demands from an advertiser to spike, or avoid printing, a story that makes the advertiser look bad.

On the other hand, a news outlet may strive to remain as unbiased as possible to increase readership and thus advertising dollars. Being strongly biased in favor of one political view may drive off many readers or viewers. Companies pay more for ads in papers with higher readership or ads on TV news programs with more viewers.

Advertisers spent $205 billion on U.S. media (TV, Internet, newspapers, and radio) in 2017. These companies and organizations may have tremendous power over what you see in the news and online.

SAYS WHO?

The people and organizations a reporter chooses to use as sources in a news article or broadcast can reflect bias. Most sources have an agenda, or a point of view they're trying to promote. From a scientist trying to protect the forest homes of local wildlife to a business owner who says that expanding their company's plant into that forest will create hundreds of jobs, there are usually multiple sides to every news story.

A good journalist will make sure to consider all sides when writing or producing a news story, even if they don't personally agree with all sides. If a reporter only focuses on the concerns over the company's expansion, they ignore the concerns of local residents in need of jobs.

When you're reading or watching a news story, consider the person who's being interviewed. Do you think their job or political ideas affect how they answer a journalist's questions?

PACK JOURNALISM

Take a look at a press conference after a bad flood or another incident or live coverage of a major fire—you'll almost certainly see several reporters crowded around the scene. One type of bias is when journalists cover stories the same way other journalists do, sometimes using the same sources. This is called pack journalism or "group think"—the tendency for reporters to share the same details instead of trying to find another way to tell a story.

COMBATING BIAS

What can journalists do to deal with bias? Reporters need to watch for it, but editors help, too. One of an editor's jobs is to guard against bias in news articles. An editor will watch for certain language and make sure the reporter used a variety of sources whose connections are well identified.

News outlets often have their own styles and rules that they use as guides to combat bias. For example, some news organizations caution against using "mailman" to describe the person who brings your mail. "Mailman" can imply gender bias—that only men are mail carriers.

To prevent corporate bias, news outlets may be transparent about their ownership. CNN, for example, will alert readers and viewers about its ties to Time Warner when reporting on the company.

A good editor can help a news story a lot. They can challenge the assumptions and biases of the reporter.

BIASED ON PURPOSE

Being **perceived** as biased isn't necessarily bad for all news outlets. Some people prefer news outlets that reflect their political views. Others may prefer to read alternative news sites, which are outlets that report on news often ignored by mainstream, or well-known, media. These alternative media sources may reflect the views of **marginalized** groups or the less powerful.

But how can an editor challenge the biases of a reporter if everyone on a newspaper staff has the same view? Just like the government, a news organization needs checks and balances. Ideally, a newsroom—the office where reporters and editors work—would be made up of people who hold a variety of political, religious, and other views. People can work together to check each other's biases and assumptions and provide new ideas.

There also should be **diversity** of all sorts in newsrooms to help avoid stereotypes and marginalization in news reports. This diversity should be reflected in stories. A reporter should make sure to interview a variety of sources. A story about women's health shouldn't have quotes only from men, for example.

Many different experiences and opinions can help the members of a newsroom recognize and avoid bias.

FALSE BALANCE

In the effort to strip news articles of bias, though, it's possible to go too far. Fair reporting is critical for good journalism, but sometimes giving balanced coverage to opposite viewpoints gives one of those viewpoints too much weight.

For example, a 1988–2002 survey of newspaper articles on global warming found that most of them included information from people who don't believe in man-made climate change. The survey also examined nearly 1,000 scientific reports from 1993 to 2003, and none disagreed with global warming. So why do journalists give equal coverage to a viewpoint that doesn't have equal scientific evidence? It could lead readers to believe the scientific community is more divided about global warming than it really is. Just because there are opposing viewpoints doesn't mean they're equal.

BREAKING NEWS

If a news article quotes two "experts" who hold opposite views on the same topics and you're not sure which one to believe, check their backgrounds. Are they both highly knowledgeable on that topic?

Journalists must use common sense when it comes to fair and balanced reporting. If one person out of 10,000 believes the sky is green, maybe their opinion shouldn't get the same amount of coverage in a story.

CAN BIAS BE GOOD?

Not all bias is bad. There are certain principles that most people in American society likely agree with, including the value of a transparent government for and by the people and those people's civil rights. When a journalist challenges a mayor or president, it's not necessarily because they disagree with that leader. It's because they believe those in power should be held **accountable** for how they lead the people.

In some ways, bias can be the basis for an entire type of reporting—investigative journalism. This is when a reporter researches a topic to uncover information previously kept hidden, such as government wrongdoing, a company's pollution cover-up, or other abuses. This can be biased because a journalist goes into the project attempting to right a wrong. This is OK as long as the final product is fair and true.

Journalists can work for months, sometimes years, on a single in-depth investigative report.

ALL THE PRESIDENT'S MEN

Perhaps one of the most well-known examples of investigative journalism involved the *Washington Post*'s reporting on an incident in the 1970s known as Watergate. Starting with a minor news story about an apparent burglary, reporters Bob Woodward and Carl Bernstein uncovered more evidence showing that President Richard Nixon and his staff were involved in a cover-up. This led to Nixon's resignation in August 1974. The story was made into a movie called *All the President's Men.*

READER BIAS

We know that news corporations, journalists, and sources can be biased. But you as a reader or viewer can also have bias. Think about where you get your news each day or what your parents watch or read. Maybe your family has a favorite channel on which you watch the local news each night. Maybe you get information from posts shared by your friends on social media.

Often, people get their information from news outlets that match their own views. A Republican may read stories on a conservative website, while a Democrat may favor a more liberal-leaning outlet. This is called confirmation bias—seeking out a spin on news that backs up your own beliefs. But if you rely only on a narrow window into the world, you may not be fully informed.

BREAKING NEWS

Reader bias can lead people to reject the credibility of articles they read just because they don't like what the articles say. It's important to check your own bias, too.

News outlets that show a strong bias are likely to be less reliable. However, consider your own biases, too.

HOW TO DETECT BIAS

With all the ways bias can seep into the news you read and watch, it may seem impossible to know whether you're getting the truth of a story. Think about who's writing the news article or producing the broadcast, who owns the news outlet, and whether there are a variety of sources from multiple sides of the story.

Is there a reason—financial, political, or otherwise—why the source may put a certain spin on a topic? Are the people interviewed for the story clearly identified? Does the news source reveal any conflicts of interest? It can seem like a lot to think about, but over time you may start to see patterns of bias—or a lack of bias—with certain reporters or news outlets.

Try researching the company that owns the TV channel your family usually watches for news. Knowing who is behind the scenes may help you detect bias in the future.

THE MORE YOU KNOW

Recognizing bias is one of the most important elements of good news literacy. A biased story means you're only getting the version of the story someone wants you to read or watch. This might not be dangerous, or you might be missing something big!

One of the best ways to combat bias is by watching or reading the news from multiple outlets. If you find yourself often agreeing with one newspaper or television station's coverage, try looking for news from an outlet you sometimes dislike. And don't just stick to the sources you see all the time. Try a different source to challenge your assumptions. Also, remember to question your own biases. We all have different ways of looking at things. It's good to see other sides!

GLOSSARY

accountable: Required to be responsible for something.

credibility: The state of being credible, or reliable and believable.

diversity: The state of having many different types, forms, or ideas.

exaggeration: The state or act of enlarging something beyond the truth.

journalism: The collecting, writing, and editing of news stories for newspapers, magazines, websites, television, or radio.

marginalize: To put something or someone, such as a group, in an unimportant or powerless position.

neutral: Not belonging to or favoring either side in an issue.

omission: Something that is left out.

perceive: To regard as being something.

prejudice: An unfair feeling of dislike for a person or group because of race or religious or political beliefs.

stereotype: An often unfair, untrue belief that people may have about all people or things of a certain kind.

unethical: Not following ethics, or rules based on what's right and what's wrong.

verify: To check whether something is true.

INDEX

WEBSITES

Due to the changing nature of Internet links, PowerKids Press has developed an online list of websites related to the subject of this book. This site is updated regularly. Please use this link to access the list: www.powerkidslinks.com/newslit/bias